GEORGIA PATRIOTS

Their Lives, Contributions, and Burial Sites

JOE FARRELL • LAWRENCE KNORR • JOE FARLEY

Mechanicsburg, PA USA

Published by Sunbury Press, Inc.
Mechanicsburg, Pennsylvania

www.sunburypress.com

Copyright © 2025 by Joe Farrell, Joe Farley, and Lawrence Knorr.
Cover Copyright © 2025 by Sunbury Press, Inc.

Sunbury Press supports copyright. Copyright fuels creativity, encourages diverse voices, promotes free speech, and creates a vibrant culture. Thank you for buying an authorized edition of this book and for complying with copyright laws by not reproducing, scanning, or distributing any part of it in any form without permission. You are supporting writers and allowing Sunbury Press to continue to publish books for every reader. For information contact Sunbury Press, Inc., Subsidiary Rights Dept., PO Box 548, Boiling Springs, PA 17007 USA or legal@sunburypress.com.

For information about special discounts for bulk purchases, please contact Sunbury Press Orders Dept. at (855) 338-8359 or orders@sunburypress.com.

To request one of our authors for speaking engagements or book signings, please contact Sunbury Press Publicity Dept. at publicity@sunburypress.com.

FIRST SUNBURY PRESS EDITION: August 2025

Set in Adobe Garamond | Interior design by Crystal Devine | Cover by Lawrence Knorr | Edited by the authors.

Publisher's Cataloging-in-Publication Data
Names: Farrell, Joe, author | Farley, Joe, author | Knorr, Lawrence, author.
Title: Georgia patriots : their lives, contributions, and burial sites / Joe Farrell Lawrence Knorr Joe Farley.
Description: First trade paperback edition. | Mechanicsburg, PA : Sunbury Press, 2025.
Summary: The individuals from Georgia who played prominent roles in the founding of the USA are detailed.
Identifiers: ISBN 979-8-88819-387-7 (softcover).
Subjects: HISTORY / United States / Revolutionary Period (1775-1800) | BIOGRAPHY & AUTOBIOGRAPHY / Political.

Designed in the USA
0 1 1 2 3 5 8 13 21 34 55

For the Love of Books!

Contents

Introduction v

Archibald Bulloch Georgia's Revolutionary Leader 1
Abraham Baldwin The Founder of the University of Georgia 6
Nathan Brownson Physician, Congressman, Governor 11
William Few The Farm Boy Who Signed the Constitution 15
Nathanael Greene Liberator of the South 20
Button Gwinnett Most Valuable Signature 26
Lyman Hall The Delegate to Congress Who Couldn't Vote 31
Edward Langworthy An Orphaned Founder 35
Edward Telfair Master of Sharon 38
George Walton The Orphaned Founder 42
Joseph Wood Pennsylvania Transplant 46

Sources 48
Index 52

Introduction

Though they abstained from the First Continental Congress in 1774, Georgia played a significant role in the American Revolution. Soon after Lexington and Concord, Georgia patriots stormed a British magazine in Savannah and ultimately chased Royal Governor Wright out of the colony. A brutal civil war followed between Patriots and Loyalists. Ultimately, the Continental Army, led by Major General Nathanael Greene, turned the tide in Georgia, propelling the rebels to eventual victory at Yorktown.

The first patriot in this book is someone who did not sign any of the founding documents of our nation. Archibald Bulloch was a charismatic leader of the revolutionary cause in Georgia from the outset. He was elected to the Second Continental Congress and simultaneously became President of Georgia. Realizing he needed to focus on his home state, rather than the nation, Bulloch returned home and missed the signing of the Declaration of Independence. However, as the first governor of the newly independent state, he received a copy of it and had it read three times a day. Unfortunately, Bulloch only lived until 1777, despite being in his forties; otherwise, he may have become more of a national figure.

Other great patriots from Georgia also followed Bulloch as governors. Button Gwinnett was the next to serve, upon Bulloch's unexpected death. George Walton and Nathan Brownson both served during the Revolution. Lyman Hall served once, while Edward Telfair served twice. George Walton also had a second term after hostilities.

Due to his impact on Georgia and his burial in Savannah, Major General Nathanael Greene is included in this volume. The war in the Southern theater turned for the better under his leadership.

As Continental Congressmen, several Georgia leaders signed the founding documents of our nation. Button Gwinnett, Lyman Hall, and George Walton signed the Declaration of Independence. Edward

Langworthy and Edward Telfair signed the Articles of Confederation. William Few and Abraham Baldwin signed the US Constitution. All told, eleven great Patriots from Georgia fill the pages of this book. While they are not close to the total of all persons who sacrificed or contributed in some way to the cause, they represent those most prominent or famous or who gave the most.

Please enjoy the retelling of our founding through the brief biographies of these citizens of Georgia. Always remember: "Poor is the nation that has no heroes, but poorer still is the nation that having heroes, fails to remember and honor them." (attributed to Marcus Tullius Cicero)

Lawrence Knorr, Ph.D.
July 2025

Archibald Bulloch
(1730–1777)

Georgia's Revolutionary Leader

Buried at Colonial Park Cemetery,
Savannah, Georgia.

Military • Continental Congress • Governor

Archibald Bulloch was a native South Carolinian who was a lawyer and politician. During the American Revolution, he was a military officer and leader of the cause in Georgia who, as governor, led the state to independence. He was the great-grandfather of Martha Bulloch Roosevelt, the mother of Theodore Roosevelt, the 26th President of the United States, and great-great-grandfather of Eleanor Roosevelt.

Bulloch was born in 1730 in Charleston, South Carolina, the son of James Bulloch (1701–1780), a planter and minister, and his wife Jean (née Stobo) Bulloch, the daughter of a Presbyterian minister, the Reverend Archibald Stobo. Bulloch was named after his maternal grandfather. James Bulloch had emigrated from Scotland circa 1728.

Bulloch was educated in Charleston in his youth and then studied law. He was admitted to the bar circa 1755 and opened a law practice. In 1757, he commissioned a lieutenant in the South Carolina militia.

In 1758, the Bulloch family moved to Georgia, where they purchased a large estate on the Savannah River across from what is now Purrysburg, South Carolina.

Illustration of Archibald Bulloch

In 1764, Bulloch moved to Savannah and married Mary De Veaux, the daughter of Judge James De Veaux. The couple ultimately had four children, including three sons and a daughter.

Bullock was elected to the colonial legislature in 1768 as a member of the Liberty Party, of which he quickly became the leader. The party was opposed to the recent oppressive measures implemented by Parliament, often triggering Royal Governor Sir James Wright to dissolve them.

On July 27, 1774, Bulloch and three key leaders of the Liberty Party, Noble Wimberly Jones, John Houston, and George Walton, met at Tondee's Tavern in Savannah to discuss the recent Parliamentary taxes on the colonies "without the consent of the people."

In January 1775, they again met at Tondee's Tavern and elected Bulloch their president. They also decided to send a delegation to the Continental Congress in Philadelphia. Bulloch, Jones, Houston, and

Archibald Bulloch (1730–1777)

Bulloch House in Savannah

John Joachim Zubly were the delegates elected on July 7, 1775. Bulloch arrived at Congress wearing homespun clothes, symbolizing Georgia's commitment to the recent Continental Association. This impressed the other delegates. John Adams praised Bulloch for his "abilities and fortitude." Bulloch was appointed to the Secret Committee regarding war supplies on November 7, 1775. Though Bulloch was elected to another term on February 2, 1776, he did not return to Congress after November 26, 1775. John Adams wrote a letter expressing his disappointment and realization that Bulloch was needed to lead back home in Georgia, "a station in which you may perhaps render more essential service to them and to America than you could here."

On September 30, 1775, back in Georgia, Bulloch was elected the President of Georgia by the Provincial Congress. George Walton was appointed as Secretary. The two of them were also members of Solomon's Lodge No. 1 of Freemasons in Savannah.

On March 2, 1776, Bulloch fought under the command of Colonel Lachlan McIntosh at the Battle of the Rice Boats. Later that month, he led a raid on Tybee Island to capture fugitive slaves who had fled to the British.

On June 20, 1776, Bulloch was named the first President and Commander-in-Chief of Georgia after Royal Governor Wright fled.

Grave of Archibald Bulloch

He regretted not being able to sign the Declaration of Independence in Philadelphia and told John Adams about his feelings. Adams was again disappointed "that you should be prevented from revisiting Philadelphia."

On August 10, 1776, Governor Bulloch received a copy of the Declaration of Independence sent by the President of Congress, John Hancock. Upon receipt, he called his council together and read it boldly to them. He then ordered it to be read three times a day to the people. Meanwhile, a salute was fired, a public dinner held, and a toast made to the new United States of America. Afterward, King George III was burned in effigy.

On February 20, 1777, Bulloch signed the new state constitution, transitioning his role from president to governor of Georgia. Two days later, while preparing for the British invasion from Florida, Bulloch died suddenly in Savannah. Some have suspected he was poisoned, though this has never been proven. Bulloch was buried in Savannah's Colonial Park Cemetery. The sign next to his grave reads, "Foremost among Georgia's revolutionary patriots stood Archibald Bulloch, whose remains rest in this vault. An early and staunch advocate of American rights, Bulloch was among the patriots who issued the call in 1774 for the first province-wide meeting of the friends of Liberty in Georgia." Bulloch County, Georgia, was named in his honor.

Son Archibald Stobo Bulloch Jr. (1775–1859) built the Archibald Bulloch House. His brother, William Bellinger Bulloch (1777–1852), later represented Georgia in the US Senate.

Great-granddaughter Martha Stewart "Mittie" (née Bulloch) Roosevelt, a Southern belle, was thought to have been one of the inspirations for Scarlett O'Hara of *Gone with the Wind*. She was also the mother of Theodore Roosevelt, the 26th President of the United States, and the paternal grandmother of Eleanor Roosevelt, the future First Lady.

The lower portion of Bulloch's tombstone reads: "Patriot, Soldier, Statesman. Georgians! Let the memory of Archibald Bulloch live in your breasts, tell your children of him, and let them tell another generation."

Abraham Baldwin
(1754–1807)

The Founder of the University of Georgia

Buried at Rock Creek Cemetery,
Washington, D.C.

U.S. Constitution

Abraham Baldwin, a native of Connecticut, was a minister, lawyer, signer of the U.S. Constitution, congressman, senator, and founder of the University of Georgia.

Abraham Baldwin was born November 22, 1754, in North Guilford, Connecticut, the son and one of five children of Michael Baldwin, a blacksmith, and his wife, Lucy (née Dudley) Baldwin. Lucy died in childbirth with the fifth child when Abraham was four. Michael was a single parent for ten years until he married Theodora Wolcott, with whom he had seven additional children, including Henry Baldwin, who became a supreme court justice.

Michael worked hard to support his large family and borrowed money to provide secondary education for young Abraham. Baldwin attended Guilford Grammar School and then Yale College in 1768 when he was 14. He was a member of the secret Linonian Society, graduating in 1772. Baldwin studied theology in preparation to become a Congregationalist minister. In 1775, he was given a license to preach and was also hired as a teacher at Yale. During the early years of the Revolution, he served as

Abraham Baldwin (1754–1807)

Abraham Baldwin

a tutor until 1779. In 1777, he enlisted as a chaplain in the Continental Army, serving with the Second Connecticut Brigade through 1783.

After the war, Yale president Ezra Stiles offered Baldwin the opportunity to be a professor of divinity, but he declined, instead pursuing law studies. He was encouraged by his former commanding officer General Nathanael Greene to follow him to Georgia, where Greene had a plantation. Baldwin did so and was admitted to the Georgia bar in 1783. Baldwin first practiced in Fairfield before moving to Augusta, Georgia. There, in 1785, he was elected to the Georgia House of Representatives where, at the urging of another transplanted New Englander, Lyman Hall, he focused on establishing an education system in the state. On May 5, 1785, Baldwin was also elected to the Continental Congress and regularly attended, except 1786.

The first college established through Baldwin's legislative efforts in the Georgia House was Franklin College, now the University of Georgia. Baldwin served as its first president from 1786 to 1801 while the institution was being formed. Wrote biographer Henry Clay White,

> [Baldwin] came to Georgia seeking neither land nor fortune. He came as a missionary in the cause of education. Happily, we may well believe, his mission, for the moment, proved ill-timed. It was not abandoned but deferred, and, in the political service to which, he, perforce, was turned, he developed a genius which was of the inestimable benefit to his State and Country.

The grave of Abraham Baldwin

Abraham Baldwin (1754–1807)

In 1787, Baldwin was appointed as a delegate to the Confederation Congress and then to the Constitutional Convention, along with William Few, William Pierce, George Walton, William Houston, and Nathaniel Pendleton. Baldwin was the most distinguished of the delegates. In September 1787 signed the U.S. Constitution. The Georgia Historical Society retains Baldwin's draft copy with his signature and handwritten notes.

Under the new government, Baldwin was elected to the U.S. House of Representatives in 1788, serving in the First Congress through the Fifth Congress from 1789 to 1799. He was then appointed by the Georgia legislature to the U.S. Senate and was re-elected in 1805 to a second six-year term. During his time in the Senate, from 1801 to 1803, he was the president pro tempore.

Back in Georgia, Franklin College finally had its first students in 1801. At that point, Baldwin resigned as president, and fellow Yale graduate Josiah Meigs took his place. The college buildings had been modeled after their alma mater, and the bulldog was adopted as the mascot, also borrowed from Yale.

On March 4, 1807, while serving as a U.S. senator from Georgia, Baldwin died. His remains were first in Rock Creek Cemetery, Washington, D.C., beside his colleague, Senator James Jackson. They were then transferred to Kalorama, another area within D.C., and finally again to Rock Creek, just down the slope from the famous Saint Gaudens' figure.

Wrote historian Ralph D. Smith in 1877,

> It is a remarkable circumstance, and an instance of assiduity almost without parallel that, during his long congressional life, he was never known to be absent a single hour during the session of congress [sic], on account of disposition or any other cause, until the week preceding his death. He was a man of great industry and talents, and his distinguished patriotism, learning, and public services shed an honor on his active state as well as that of his adoption.

GEORGIA PATRIOTS

The *Georgia Historical Quarterly* concluded in 1919,

> During the violent agitation of parties which have disturbed the repose of public men in this country for the last ten years, [Baldwin] has always been moderate but firm; relaxing nothing in his republican principles but retaining all possible charity for his former friends who may have abandoned theirs. He has lived without reproach and has probably died without an enemy.

Abraham Baldwin has been honored in many ways. Baldwin counties in Georgia and Alabama are named after him. His name also adorns Abraham Baldwin Agricultural College in Tifton, Georgia, and Abraham Baldwin Middle School in Guilford, Connecticut. There are Baldwin streets in Madison, Wisconsin, and Athens, Georgia. A statue of Baldwin was erected on the campus of the University of Georgia, and the U.S. Postal Service issued a stamp in his honor as part of the Great Americans series.

Nathan Brownson
(1742–1796)

Physician, Congressman, Governor

Buried at Midway Cemetery,
Midway, Georgia.

Continental Congress • Governor

Nathan Brownson was a Connecticut physician who moved to Georgia, where he became a state legislator and Continental Congressman. Near the end of the American Revolution, he was the Governor of Georgia.

Brownson was born on May 14, 1742, in Woodbury, near Hartford, Connecticut, the son of Timothy Brownson and his wife, Abigail (née Jenner) Brownson.

Brownson was schooled by private tutors in his youth before attending Yale. He graduated in 1761 with a medical degree and practiced medicine in Woodbury.

On June 29, 1769, Brownson married Abigail Lewis. In 1774, after corresponding with his friend, Dr. James Dunwoody, of St. John's Parish, Georgia, Brownson traveled there. Soon after, he and his wife moved to Riceboro, near the town of Midway, Liberty County, where he worked a 500-acre plantation. Abigail died soon after they moved to Georgia, and Brownson next married Elizabeth Dunham Martin, a widow, on September 2, 1774.

On July 4, 1775, the provincial congress met in Savannah to discuss the issues of the Revolution. Brownson and Lyman Hall were two of

Nathan Brownson

eleven delegates from the parish to attend. Back home, Elizabeth died in 1775, likely due to childbirth. Brownson next married Elizabeth McLean in 1776, also a widow, with whom he had two children.

On October 9, 1776, Brownson joined Lyman Hall as appointees to the Second Continental Congress.

Brownson's service in the Continental Congress lasted from January 4 to May 1, 1777, in Philadelphia, and then from August 23 to October 9, 1777, as the Congress relocated to Lancaster and subsequently to York, Pennsylvania.

As the Revolutionary War progressed, the focus switched to the Southern Theater. After the British were expelled from Augusta in June 1781, there was chaos and factional disputes in Georgia. The Continental Congress sent Brownson to Georgia as a brigadier to assist in bringing order. He was initially made Speaker of the House in the state assembly, but a compromise was arranged whereby John Twiggs became a brigadier general and Brownson became the governor of the state, succeeding Stephen Heard.

Nathan Brownson (1742–1796)

Brownson's term lasted only from August 17, 1781, until January 3, 1782. As one of his acts as governor, he congratulated General Nathanael Greene for his efforts to restore the state's government. Brownson put out a call to all men to return to their homes in the state or pay triple the tax that would be due. He also worked to settle the Creek Indians, who had been threatening American soldiers and property. John Martin then succeeded Brownson.

Next for Brownson was to revisit his medical background. On June 6, 1782, he was appointed as the deputy purveyor for the Southern Hospitals for the Continental Army.

Brownson spent the years after the war as a justice of the peace, a commissioner for a new capital, and a member of the state's Constitutional Convention. In 1788, he was elected to the Georgia House of Representatives and rose to the speaker's chair. He was also appointed to assist in the writing of a new state constitution. When that document was ratified, creating a state senate, Brownson was elected to that body, serving from 1790 to 1791, rising to president of the senate. Around this time, he was also involved as a trustee in the formation of Franklin College, which later became the University of Georgia.

Brownson died at his Riceboro plantation in Liberty County, Georgia, on November 6, 1796, at age 54. He was buried in Midway Cemetery in Midway, Georgia. *The Federal Gazette* of Baltimore, Maryland, announced Brownson's death, then noted that his "various talents as a statesman, philosopher and physician, have placed him in the list of distinguished characters. His expiring moments were marked with that peculiar firmness of mind which attended him through life, and his last words, delivered in whispers, were more sublimely eloquently than all the studied declamation of the pulpit. 'The scene (said he) is now closing, the business of life is nearly over; I have, like the rest of my fellow creatures, been guilty of foibles; but I trust to the mercy of my God to pardon them, and to his justice, and to reward my good deeds.' By his family, by his friends, who knew him, his death will be long lamented."

Historian James F. Cook later wrote: "A friend who was well acquainted with Dr. Brownson and his wife related that Mrs. Brownson, though a good and faithful wife, was not always prompt in responding to the requests of her husband. On occasion, Dr. Brownson playfully said to her: 'Have a care; if you do not acquiesce in my wish, when I am dead, I will come back and plague you.' Years later, after Brownson's death, his widow, when brushing from her nose some vexatious fly or annoying insect, was heard to exclaim, 'Go away, I tell you, Doctor Brownson, and stop bothering me."

William Few
(1748–1828)

The Farm Boy Who Signed the Constitution

Buried at Saint Paul's Episcopal Cemetery,
Augusta, Georgia.

Military • Confederation Congress • US Constitution

Founders like the subject of this chapter were, pun intended, few and far between. This founder was born into a poor farming family. His parents made a modest living raising tobacco. His educational opportunities were limited, but he made the most of what he learned from them. He had a family member hanged by loyalists. He overcame hardships and rose to become a political power. He demonstrated his ability to both lead and organize during the Revolutionary War. He represented Georgia at the 1787 Constitutional Convention, where he proudly added his signature to the document that the gathering produced. He would serve as one of the first United States senators from Georgia. His name was William Few.

Few was born on June 8, 1748, in Baltimore County, Maryland. His father was a Quaker and his mother a Catholic. They supported the family by farming, but in the 1750s, a series of droughts pushed them and many of their neighbors to near ruin. These people abandoned their holdings and moved to the southern frontier of North Carolina.

While prosperous farmers were able to provide for the education of their children, such was not the case with Few. As described by Denise

Illustration of William Few

Kiernan and Joseph D'Agnese in their work *Signing Their Rights Away*, Few himself recalled an experience at a country school as being filled with "terror and anxiety" because of a teacher he absolutely hated. After the family moved, his second and last year of schooling was more enjoyable and provided Few with a love of reading and learning that would serve as a tremendous influence on his life.

When Few was sixteen, his family moved to Hillsborough. There, the Few's became involved with a group called the Regulators, a movement that resulted from the political and economic restrictions frontier farmers faced. These restrictions were imposed by merchants and local politicians. Many of their politicians and local sheriffs were corrupt and sought to exploit the farmers and the working class whenever possible. The protests by the Regulators grew and resulted in a confrontation on May 16, 1771, known as the Battle of Alamance, when 1,000 militia troops led by the Royal Governor William Tryon crushed the uprising. Few's brother James was captured and hanged. The family farm was destroyed, and Few's father, now being pressured by creditors, fled to Georgia. Few, his passion for American freedom fueled by the incident, stayed behind to settle his family's financial affairs and sell their property.

While in Hillsborough, Few also joined the militia and formed a volunteer company. He attended meetings to gain a deeper understanding of the conflict between the colonies and the mother country. As the American Revolution grew closer, Few wrote, "I felt the spirit of an American, and without much investigation of the justice of her cause, I resolved to defend it."

After handling his family's affairs, Few joined them near Augusta, Georgia. He joined the militia there and rose to the rank of lieutenant colonel. In 1777, his political life began when he was elected to the convention that would establish the Georgia constitution. He served in the state's first legislature and on the governor's advisory council.

In 1778, Few was called to active duty as Georgia prepared for a possible invasion by British and Loyalist troops stationed in Florida. While they did temporarily hold off the opposition, the trip was far from a success. Many Americans fell ill in the swamps. Only half of the American troops survived. By year's end, a sudden invasion by the British captured Savannah. By 1779, Few was second in command of a regiment that eventually forced the English to abandon Augusta. Few emerged from the southern fighting with a reputation as a skilled administrator and logistics expert. He was also recognized as a bold commander who could pick the time and place to engage small enemy parties. He also demonstrated that he possessed the physical strength to endure the hardships that came with fighting a guerrilla war.

In 1780, he was elected to serve in the Continental Congress. He would be in Congress for less than a year. When General Nathanael Greene drove the British out of Georgia, he returned there to assist in reassembling the state's government. He served in the state legislature and practiced law. He was a self-taught lawyer who later wrote that he had "never spent one hour in the office of an attorney to prepare for the business, nor did I know anything of the practice."

In 1786, Few once again represented Georgia in the Continental Congress. Congress was now meeting in New York City, so when, in 1787, his state sent him as one of its representatives to the Constitutional

Convention in Philadelphia, this resulted in a number of commutes between the two cities. He was one of the very few representatives at the convention in Philadelphia who came from what would be considered a working-class family farm background. He still managed to make an impression. As told in the aforementioned work, *Signing Their Rights Away*, Georgia delegate William Pierce wrote, "Mr. Few possesses a strong natural Genius, and from application has acquired some knowledge of legal matters; he practices at the bar of Georgia, and speaks tolerably well in the legislature. He has twice served as a Member of Congress, fulfilling his duties with fidelity to his state and honor to himself. In his work *1787: The Grand Convention*, historian Clinton Rossiter wrote that although he never spoke at the convention, Few made his presence felt by voting the right way at critical moments. Few would sign and then work to ratify the Constitution.

A few then served as one of Georgia's first U.S. senators. Here he became a supporter of Thomas Jefferson and an opponent of Alexander Hamilton. He strongly opposed the creation of the First Bank of the United States. He hoped to retire from public service in 1793 but was convinced by friends to serve another term in the state legislature. In 1796, he was appointed as a federal judge for the Georgia circuit. He earned a reputation as a fair jurist. He was a proud supporter of formal education, having been largely denied it himself, and was a founding trustee of the University of Georgia.

His wife, a native New Yorker, convinced him to move to the city in 1799. Here, he made a living in banking, where he served as the president of the City Bank of New York. He was also elected to serve in the New York

Grave of William Few

William Few (1748–1828)

State Assembly. He also served as inspector of the state prisons, as a state commissioner of loans and as a city alderman.

When he finally retired at the age of sixty-eight, his wealth was estimated to exceed $100,000, which would amount to more than $2.5 million today. This was quite an accomplishment considering his humble beginnings. He died at the home of his daughter at the age of eighty. He was originally buried in New York, but his remains were later moved to St. Paul's Church in Augusta, Georgia.

Nathanael Greene
(1742 – 1786)
Liberator of the South

Buried at Johnson Square,
Savannah, Georgia.

Military

Nathanael Greene, a native of Rhode Island, was a major general during the American Revolution. He was one of three men, besides George Washington and Henry Knox, to serve the entire duration of the war. Greene was second in command to only Washington, and towards the end of the war turned the tide in the British-ravaged south.

Nathanael Greene was born on "Forge Farm" in Potowomut, Rhode Island, on August 7, 1742. He was the son of Nathanael Greene (1707-1768), a Quaker farmer and smith. He was descended from John Greene Sr. and Samuel Gorton who were both early settlers of Warwick, Rhode Island. His mother was Mary Mott, the second wife of Nathanael senior. Greene was mostly self-educated and influenced by Reverend Ezra Stiles, who was later a president of Yale University.

Around the time of his father's death, Greene moved to Coventry, Rhode Island and took charge of the family's foundry. There he also established a public school and was chosen to the Rhode Island Assembly, to which he was re-elected several times. He married Catharine Littlefield in July 1774 with whom he had six children who survived infancy.

Nathanael Greene (1742–1786)

Original portrait of Nathanael Greene painted from life in 1783 by Charles Willson Peale.

Though a Quaker, he eschewed that faith's commitment to pacifism in the face of American independence. In August 1774, Greene helped organize a local militia and began reading extensively about military tactics. In December, he was on a committee to revise militia laws. This focus on the military led to his expulsion from the Quakers.

On May 8, 1775, Greene was promoted to major general of the Rhode Island Army of Observation that formed in response to the siege of Boston. The Continental Congress appointed him a brigadier general in the Continental Army the following month. Washington assigned Greene to command the city of Boston after it was evacuated by the British in March 1776.

On August 9, 1776, Greene was promoted to major general and was given command of the Continental Army on Long Island. He led the construction of entrenchments and fortifications but was prevented by illness from taking part in the Battle of Long Island. Greene advocated

Equestrian statue of Nathanael Greene at Guilford Court House Battlefield (photo by Lawrence Knorr).

for a retreat from New York City and was then stationed on the New Jersey side of the Hudson. After the Americans retreated, Greene commanded one of the two columns at the Battle of Trenton. He urged to press immediately on to Princeton but was rebuffed by his peers.

During the Philadelphia campaign, at the Battle of Brandywine, Greene commanded the reserves. At Germantown, his troops distinguished themselves but were late to the field. In March of 1778, Washington appointed him Quartermaster General at Valley Forge with the understanding he would retain command of troops in the field. Greene was in command of the right wing at Monmouth in late June of 1778.

In August of 1778, Greene returned to his home state of Rhode Island with Lafayette to command the land forces in cooperation with French Admiral d'Estaing at the successful Battle of Rhode Island. Back in New Jersey in June of 1780, Greene was in command at the Battle of Springfield, putting an end to British ambitions in the north. In August, he resigned as Quartermaster General after a long dispute with Congress regarding how the army should be administered and supplied. Washington appointed Greene commander at West Point where he presided over the condemnation of Major John André on September 29, 1780.

On October 5, 1780, Washington appointed Greene as commander of the southern theater, giving him charge of all troops from Delaware

Nathanael Greene (1742–1786)

to Georgia. He took command at Hillsborough, North Carolina, on December 3, 1780, replacing Horatio Gates. Greene decided to divide his troops in the face of a superior force under Cornwallis. At Kings Mountain in 1780, Colonel William Campbell captured or killed the entire British force. At Cowpens, on January 17, 1781, General Daniel Morgan captured or killed 90% of the British forces. With over 800 prisoners in tow, the Americans began a strategic retreat to draw Cornwallis out, leveraging light cavalry to harass the enemy. The force successfully crossed the Dan River ahead of the British and reached safety in Virginia. Some have referred to this one of the most masterful military achievements of all time.

Now strengthened by reinforcements, Greene's army re-crossed the Dan River and faced Cornwallis at the Battle of Guilford Court House on ground chosen by Greene. As the Americans were turning the British flank, Cornwallis ordered the cannons to fire on his own troops and the Americans. This repulsed the attack, though Cornwallis lost as many of his own as his enemy. Greene then ordered a tactical retreat that further battered and exhausted Cornwallis. The British withdrew towards Wilmington, North Carolina, while Greene now turned towards the liberation of the low country of South Carolina, achieved by June 1781. After the Battle of Eutaw Springs, the British were now forced to the coast where Greene eventually pinned them at Charleston until the end of the war.

Regarding the Southern Campaign, though defeated in every pitched battle by a superior enemy, Greene managed to divide, elude, and tire his opponent through long marches. The Americans chipped away at a British force that was not being reinforced. Others in the campaign were Polish engineer Tadeusz Kościuszko, cavalry officers Henry ("Light-Horse Harry") Lee and William Washington, and partisan leaders Thomas Sumter, Andrew Pickens, Elijah Clarke, and Francis Marion. In the end, Greene had liberated the southern states from British control. When the Treaty of Paris ended the war, British forces controlled a couple of southern coastal cities, but Greene controlled the rest.

After the war, Greene was an original member of the Rhode Island Society of the Cincinnati, serving as president until his death. Several of the southern states granted him lands and money. He sold most of the land to pay war debts associated with his role as Quartermaster General. He kept the "Mulberry Grove" plantation granted to him near Savannah, Georgia.

Grave of Nathanael Greene beneath Johnson Square in Savannah, Georgia (photo by Joe Farrell).

He was offered the post of Secretary of War by President Washington but declined.

Greene died at "Mulberry Grove" on June 19, 1786, at the age of only 43. He was initially interred at the Graham Vault in Colonial Park Cemetery in Savannah. On October 14, 1902, his remains were moved to a monument in Johnson Square in Savannah.

There are many memorials to Nathanael Greene:

- There are many cities, counties, and parks named after him across the country.
- Ships: four Coast Guard cutters, a James Madison-class nuclear submarine, an Army cargo ship, a Liberty class steam merchant, and a 128-foot Army tug which is still in service today.

Nathanael Greene (1742–1786)

- A large portrait hangs in the Rhode Island State House, and a statue stands outside the building.
- A cenotaph to him stands in the Old Forge Burial Ground in Warwick.
- His statue, with that of Roger Williams, represents the state of Rhode Island in the National Hall of Statuary in the Capitol.
- In Washington, there is a bronze equestrian statue by Henry Kirke Brown at the center of Stanton Park.

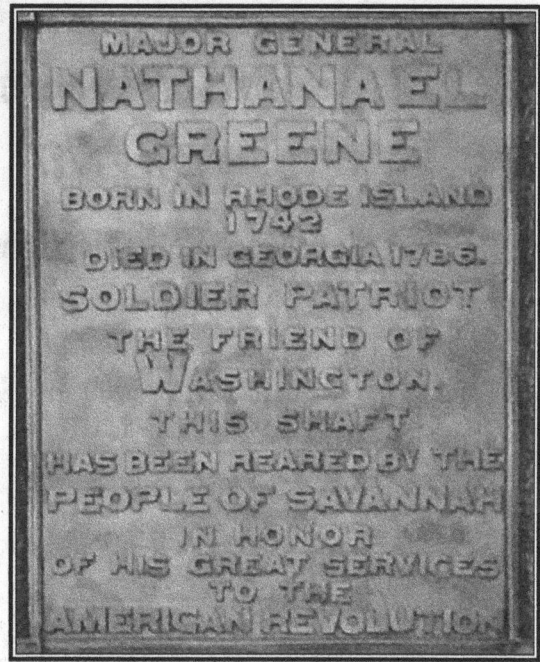

Detail from Nathanael Greene's monument (photo by Joe Farrell).

- A small statue by Lewis Iselin, Jr. is outside the Philadelphia Museum of Art.
- An equestrian statue designed by Francis H. Packer at the site of the Battle of Guilford Courthouse.
- A statue stands in the middle of the traffic circle between Greene Street and McGee Street in downtown Greensboro.
- Greeneville, Tennessee and Greene County, Tennessee are named after him.
- The city of Greenville, South Carolina, also named for him, unveiled a statue designed by T. J. Dixon and James Nelson at the corner of South Main and Broad Streets.
- A bronze statue of Greene by sculptor Chas Fagan is in St. Clair Park, in Greensburg, Pennsylvania.
- A statue is in Valley Forge National Military Park, Pennsylvania.
- The Nathanael Greene Homestead is in Coventry, Rhode Island.

Button Gwinnett
(1735 – 1777)

Most Valuable Signature

Buried at Colonial Park Cemetery,
Savannah, Georgia.

Declaration of Independence

The story of Button Gwinnett is unusual. He was born in England where he failed as a merchant. He came to America for what seemed a better opportunity and a fresh start but he failed as a merchant in Charleston and then again in Savannah. He bought land in Georgia and tried life as a planter but this too failed. A late convert to the independence cause, he was elected to the Continental Congress in 1776, signed the Declaration of Independence, and was killed in a duel with a political rival shortly thereafter at the age of forty-five.

Button Gwinnett was born in Gloucestershire County to a Welsh father and an English mother. There are conflicting reports on the exact date of his birth but he was baptized on April 10, 1735, in St. Catherine's Church in Gloucester. Not much is known of his formal education, but he was apprenticed to a merchant in the city of Bristol. He married Ann Bourne in 1757. He was the sole owner of the brig *Nancy*, but his business proved unsuccessful and his ship was seized and sold to pay his debts. Seeking opportunity, he and his family set out for America arriving in Charleston in 1765. He set himself up as a trader but after a

Button Gwinnett (1735-1777)

Portrait of Button Gwinnett by Nathaniel Hone the Elder.

few years he sold all his merchandise and moved to Savannah where he opened a store. This venture also failed and he bought a large tract of land on St. Catherine's Island and became a planter.

Around this time, Gwinnett befriended Lyman Hall, a future signer of the Declaration, who had re-settled in Georgia from New England. Through his friendship with Hall, Gwinnett developed an interest in politics and in 1769 was elected to the Georgia Colonial Assembly. More financial problems limited his involvement in public service over the next few years. In 1772, he acquired property in St. John's Parish but in 1773 creditors seized his properties. He was allowed to continue living in his home there for the rest of his life.

Prior to 1775, Gwinnett was known to be a patriotic citizen but he felt successful resistance to so mighty a power as that of England appeared extremely doubtful. Lyman Hall helped persuade him to change his views and he soon became an open advocate of strong and decided action to secure American rights. As a result, he was elected to attend a provincial assembly on January 20, 1776, in Savannah. He was elected by that body to represent Georgia in the Continental Congress. He took his seat in the Congress in May and while he is not known as a major player in the debates, he voted for independence on July 2, for the formal declaration on July 4, and signed his name to the Declaration on August 2.

In October 1776, Gwinnett was again elected to the Georgia assembly and named Speaker and re-elected to the Continental Congress. During his service in the Congress, he was a candidate for a brigadier general position of the 1st Regiment in the Continental Army but lost out to Lachlan McIntosh. Gwinnett was sorely disappointed and embittered and regarded McIntosh as an enemy from that day forward.

In the Georgia Assembly, Gwinnett played an important role in drafting the state's first constitution. When the President (Governor) of Georgia, Archibald Bulloch, died in March 1777, he was appointed to the vacant position by the Assembly's Executive Council. In this position, he was the Commander-In-Chief of Georgia's Militia and he used his power to undermine the leadership of McIntosh. Gwinnett took an active role which caused dissension in the ranks and McIntosh was treated with disrespect by some officers and soldiers. McIntosh had planned an expedition into eastern Florida to secure Georgia's southern border but Governor Gwinnett took over the planning of the expedition and would have led the troops himself but was prevented from doing so due to his position as head of the Provincial Assembly. Instead, he appointed one of McIntosh's subordinates as the commander of the expedition.

The expedition was a failure and Gwinnett and McIntosh publicly blamed each other. Gwinnett was charged with malfeasance but was cleared of all wrongdoing by an inquest. However, he lost his bid for re-election as Governor. On May 1, 1777, Lachlan McIntosh addressed the Georgia assembly denouncing Gwinnett in the harshest terms, calling him "a scoundrel and a lying rascal." Gwinnett called on McIntosh and demanded an apology but McIntosh refused. The consequence was a challenge to a duel sent by Gwinnett and accepted by McIntosh.

Button Gwinnett (1735 – 1777)

They met in the small town of Thunderbolt, near Savannah on May 16, 1777, and fought at a distance of only twelve feet. They were both severely wounded. Gwinnett died of a gangrene infection on May 19 at the age of 45. McIntosh quickly recovered and was charged with murder but acquitted. He went on to live until 1806. Fearing Gwinnett's allies would take revenge on McIntosh, George Washington ordered him to report to Continental Army headquarters in Valley Forge, Pennsylvania, where he spent the winter.

A large beautiful monument in Colonial Park Cemetery marks the site of Gwinnett's grave, though no one is exactly sure it is his. The Colonial Park Cemetery had not been well-maintained into the 1840s and many markers were lost. In 1848, when patriotic citizens wished to move his grave to be with those of Lyman Hall and George Walton beneath the

The alleged grave of Button Gwinnett at Colonial Park Cemetery in Savannah, Georgia (photo by Joe Farrell).

Georgia Signers' Monument in Augusta, Georgia, Gwinnett's remains could not be located. In 1957, retired school principal Arthur Funk began a search for Gwinnett. He located a marker that contained clues linking to Gwinnett and with the help of a New York archaeologist (and permission of the city) began an excavation. Bones were located in the grave that were believed to be Gwinnett's. Controversy raged for several years as the Smithsonian and others weighed in. Some thought the femur had evidence of a musket ball tied to Gwinnett's fatal wounds. Others said the bone was damaged after burial. Some, including the archaeologist, thought the bones were that of a woman. Nonetheless, after much debate, the bones were reinterred in the cemetery and a new monument erected to Gwinnett noting that his bones are "believed to be" here.

Button Gwinnett is memorialized in many places, such as Gwinnett County, Georgia, the Button Gwinnett Elementary School in Hinesville, Georgia, and the Button Gwinnett Chapter of the Sons of the American Revolution in Lawrenceville, Georgia. There is a large monument in Augusta, Georgia to the three Georgia signers of the Declaration of Independence and in 1955 his bust was one of the first three placed in the Georgia Hall of Fame. Gwinnett's signature is considered among the most valuable of historical autographs in the world. This is due to collectors attempting to obtain a complete set of the signers of the Declaration of Independence, as well as his signature being a rarity. Only fifty-one examples of his signature are known to exist. In 1979 a letter signed by Gwinnett brought $100,000 at a New York auction. In 2010 a document bearing his signature sold for $722,000.

Lyman Hall
(1724–1790)

The Delegate to Congress Who Couldn't Vote

Buried at Courthouse Grounds,
Augusta, Georgia.

Continental Congress • Declaration of Independence

This founder was born in the north but represented a southern colony in the Continental Congress. He was a clergyman and a physician. He was a fierce proponent of American independence. As such, he took pleasure in affixing his signature to the Declaration of Independence. Actor Jonathan Moore portrayed him in the 1972 movie *1776*. His name was Lyman Hall.

Hall was born on April 12, 1724, in Wallingford, Connecticut. His father was a minister named John Hall. His mother, Mary, was the daughter of the Reverend Samuel Street. He graduated from Yale in 1747 with the intention of becoming a minister, too. He began his ministry in 1749, but things did not go smoothly. He was serving in the pulpit of Stratfield Parish, and he found himself at odds with his congregation. In 1751, he was dismissed based on charges involving his moral character. According to one biographer, these allegations "Were supported by proof and also by his own confession." He continued to preach for two more years, filling in when a pulpit was vacant. At that point, he decided to change his career to medicine, and he apprenticed with a physician.

In 1752, Hall married Abigail Burr. His bride passed away roughly a year later. In 1757, he married Mary Osborne, with whom he had one

Illustration of Lyman Hall

son. The Hall family then decided to move south. First to South Carolina and then to St. John's Parish along the Georgia coast. Here, Hall became involved in founding Sunbury, which later developed into a seaport hub. As told by Denise Kiernan and Joseph D'Agnese in their work *Signing Their Lives Away*, the swampy, malarial messes that needed to be drained in the area produced enough disease-carrying mosquitoes to keep Dr. Hall quite busy. He became one of the leading citizens in Sunbury and soon set up a plantation, Hall's Knoll, near the town.

Like Hall, many of Sunbury's residents were transplanted northerners. These people had ties to both friends and families in the north, and as a result, Sunbury became a supporter of the patriot cause. Georgia was one of the most remote colonies, and the majority felt that the relationship with England was not a threat. In fact, Georgia was the only colony that did not send any representatives to the First Continental Congress. Georgia also rejected the Congress recommendation for the Continental Association, which called for an embargo on trade with the mother country.

Hall and most of the people in St. John's Parish grew frustrated with the leadership in Georgia. Wanting representation in Congress, the

Lyman Hall (1724–1790)

Parish, under Hall's leadership, contacted South Carolina with the goal of becoming part of that colony. South Carolina refused the offer.

In March of 1775, St. John's withdrew from the Georgia legislative body and held their own convention. They voted to send their own delegate to the Second Continental Congress, sending Hall as their representative. Arriving in Philadelphia that May, representing a single Georgia county, Congress was confused as to what Hall's place should be. Wanting Georgia to be represented in some manner, Hall was admitted as

The Signers' Monument in Augusta, Georgia, honors three patriots.

a nonvoting member. In July, after the battles at Lexington and Concord, the mood in Georgia changed. The colony acknowledged Hall's place in Congress and sent four other delegates to join him.

The Georgia delegates received no specific instructions. They were simply advised to do what they believed necessary for the common good. When the time came, Georgia voted for independence, and Hall was one of three Georgia representatives who signed their names on the Declaration of Independence.

In 1778, the British had turned their attention to the southern states. In January of 1779, Sunbury was burned, and the British destroyed Hall's plantation. Hall and his family fled north, back to Connecticut. He returned to Georgia when the English evacuated in 1782. He once again practiced medicine as he worked to repair his damaged finances.

In January of 1783, Hall was elected governor of the state. In this position, he worked on improving the economy, made treaties with the Cherokee Indians and advocated the chartering of a state university. His efforts resulted in the establishment of the University of Georgia. Upon leaving the governor's office, he resumed his medical practice.

In 1790, Hall moved to Burke County, where he purchased another plantation. Within a year of the move, he passed away on October 19 at the age of sixty-six. He was initially laid to rest on his plantation but later his remains were moved to Augusta. He is now buried beneath a monument honoring Georgia's signers of the Declaration.

Grave of Lyman Hall

Edward Langworthy
(1738 – 1802)

An Orphaned Founder

He was initially buried at the Old Episcopal Church in Baltimore, Maryland. The church was demolished in 1891, and the location of his remains is unknown.

Articles of Confederation

This founder's parents were likely among the first colonists shipped to Georgia. This conclusion is because he was born within five years of James Oglethorpe recruiting those in poorhouses and debtors' prisons to be the first to settle in the region. It appears his parents died when he was very young as he was raised in the Bethesda Orphan House in Savannah. Despite these challenging beginnings, he would rise to represent Georgia in the Continental Congress during the American Revolution and sign the Articles of Confederation. This document officially united the thirteen colonies as a country. Described by Burton Alva Knokle in *The Georgia Historical Quarterly* as a patriot, teacher, statesman, editor, writer, historian, and eminent citizen of two states, this founder's name was Edward Langworthy.

Edward Langworthy

Langworthy was born in Savannah circa 1738. It appears his parents died when he was relatively young as he was raised and educated in Savannah's Bethesda Orphan House. He took his studies seriously as he became one of the instructors at the orphanage. At one point, he took out an advertisement in a Georgia newspaper which read, "The subscriber having taken a convenient House, proposes to board eight young gentlemen at 22 per annum, and to instruct them in the Latin and Greek Languages. The greatest care will be taken to improve them in the English language and to accustom them to a just and agreeable manner in pronunciation and reading. Young ladies may be taught English Grammar, Writing, &c. privately." It appears that teaching as a profession appealed to him since he would take up the profession again later in life.

In 1774, when the fires that became the American Revolution were already burning, Langworthy remained loyal to the British crown, as evidenced by his signing the Loyalist protest of the Savannah Resolutions. His Loyalist leanings did not last long as, within a year, he reversed his position entirely and was chosen secretary to the Revolutionary body known as the Council of Safety. Two months later, he became a member of the Georgia Provincial Congress, where he was appointed secretary of that body. In this position, Langworthy signed the initial delegates' credentials to represent Georgia at the Continental Congress meeting in Philadelphia. Among the credentials he signed was one for a good friend of his, Button Gwinnett. Gwinnett would affix his signature to the Declaration of Independence.

On June 7, 1777, the Georgia legislature elected Langworthy to serve as a delegate to the Continental Congress. As a representative from Georgia, he signed the Articles of Confederation on July 24, 1778. The Articles formally brought the thirteen states together, forming the United States of America. He was not a vocal member of Congress as he is not recorded as ever having made a motion though he did second on two occasions. He was among the representatives who spent time in York, Pennsylvania, when the Congress was moved there after the British army occupied Philadelphia. Based on a letter he wrote at the time, he had little liking for the city. After completing his service in Congress, Langworthy returned to Georgia, where he may well have begun the research on the state's first history, which he would work on for years but never complete. His papers involving this project have never been recovered.

In 1785, Langworthy moved to Baltimore, where he became part owner and the editor of the *Maryland Journal & Baltimore Advertiser*. The newspaper flourished and proved to be a successful business venture. In one open letter to the paper's readers, Langworthy and his co-owner, William Goddard, stated, "It would perhaps be to little Purpose to descant on the many Advantages derived from the Art of Printing; that the present Age is esteemed an Enlightened One, and that we are in the enjoyment of Political Independence, and Perfect Freedom in the important Concerns of Religion, may, in a great Degree, be ascribed to the Liberty of the Press."

When Langworthy was busy with his newspaper, the Baltimore religious heads of the Catholic, Episcopalian, and Presbyterian churches established the Baltimore Academy. The institution's purpose was to provide the young men in the area an opportunity to pursue a higher education without leaving home. Langworthy was chosen to head the school where he also taught the classics. It is not clear how long he labored at the Academy. It is known that he sold his interest in the newspaper on January 1, 1787, and that in March of that year, he completed his memoir of General Charles Lee. In 1792 this work was published in both New York and London.

In 1795, Langworthy was appointed to the post of Baltimore's Clerk of Customs. He would serve in this position until he died on November 2, 1802. He had impressed many in the Baltimore area relative to his conduct and life in his adopted second city.

His obituary stated, "After a severe illness of six days . . . the spirit of Edward Langworthy, Esq. deputy naval officer of the port of Baltimore, took its flight for 'another and a better world.' To eulogize the defunct is not the intention of the writer of this paragraph, suffice it to say, that his public and private walks in life were such as many may endeavor to imitate, but a few will attain to equal perfection."

Langworthy was laid to rest in the yard of Baltimore's Old Episcopal Church. That church was demolished in 1891, and the records of the graveyard were lost.

Edward Telfair
(1738 – 1807)

Master of Sharon

Buried at Bonaventure Cemetery,
Savannah, Georgia.

Articles of Confederation • Governor

Edward Telfair was a native of Scotland who moved to Virginia, Nova Scotia, North Carolina, and then Georgia, where he became a merchant involved in the slave trade. He was also a state legislator, Continental Congressman, and two-time governor of the state. While in the Continental Congress, he signed the Articles of Confederation.

Telfair was born, according to most sources, in 1735, on the family's farm near Kirkcudbright, Galloway, Scotland. The names of his parents are no longer known. He attended the local grammar school and later studied commercial trade.

According to most sources, Telfair, a young man in 1758, was an agent for a commission house that sent him to the colonies, where he first settled in Virginia. He then hopped to Halifax, Nova Scotia and North Carolina, before joining his brother in Savannah, Georgia, in 1766. Telfair partnered with Basil Cowper in their own commission house which was very successful. The primary focus of the operation was the importation of enslaved people. Telfair wrote about methods to manage enslaved people best and the challenges owners faced, including

Edward Telfair (1738–1807)

Edward Telfair

runaways, mortality, dealing with those who were closely related, and relations between whites and freedmen.

In 1768, Telfair was elected to Georgia's Commons House of Assembly while also serving in lower-level offices in Savannah.

In 1774, Telfair married Sarah Gibbons, age 16, at her mother's plantation, Sharon, west of Savannah. The couple ultimately had six children, three sons and three daughters.

When hostilities began with Great Britain, Telfair sided with the rebels. He participated in the "general meeting of inhabitants" in Savannah on August 10, 1774, which passed several resolutions in protest.

The following year, Telfair was appointed to the Georgia Committee of Safety and the Provincial Congress. After the Battle of Lexington and Concord, Telfair participated in an attack on the British garrison at Savannah to seize arms and ammunition on May 11, 1775. In 1776, he was added to the Georgia Committee of Intelligence.

Next, Telfair was elected to the Continental Congress four times: February 26, 1778; January 11, 1780; August 17, 1781; and February 10, 1782. Having arrived in Philadelphia on July 8, 1778, he, Edward Langworthy, and John Walton signed the Articles of Confederation on behalf of Georgia. He then served in the Congress between July 13 and

November 16, 1778, after the Congress had returned from York. Telfair was rarely mentioned in the correspondence of the Congress and appears to have been uninvolved in most of the debates. His service ended in January 1783.

The following month, February 1783, Georgia commissioned Telfair to negotiate a treaty with the Chickamauga Cherokee Indians in a bid to end the Cherokee-American wars. He also helped settle a boundary dispute between North and South Carolina and attended Georgia's ratification of the Articles of Confederation.

On January 9, 1786, Telfair was elected as the 19th governor of Georgia and the first under the new state constitution, succeeding Samuel Elbert, serving until January 9, 1787, when he was succeeded by George Mathews.

In 1788, Telfair served as a delegate to the state constitutional convention and represented Burke County at the ratifying convention of the US Constitution in 1789. Telfair was one of only twelve people to receive electoral votes in the nation's first presidential election.

On November 9, 1790, Telfair was again elected to the governor's office, succeeding George Walton. He then served two full terms through

Grave of Edward Telfair

November 7, 1793. During his tenure, he dealt with Native tribes and was involved in illegal land sales to speculators as part of the Yazoo land scandal.

In 1794, Telfair was unsuccessful in his attempt to run for the US Senate from Georgia, losing to incumbent James Gunn. He then retired from public service until he was appointed as a justice in the Inferior Court in Chatham County, Georgia, on February 14, 1799.

Telfair died on September 17, 1807, and was initially interred in the family vault on the Sharon Plantation. Soon after, Telfair County, Georgia, was named in his honor.

Son Thoms Telfair (1780–1818) was a member of the US House of Representatives for two terms from 1813 to 1817.

Decades later, Telfair's remains were transferred to a large sarcophagus at Bonaventure Cemetery in Savannah. It was engraved "Edward Telfair of Georgia, who Died Sept. 17, 1807. Aged 64." This age is likely in error because it would infer his birth year as 1743. Most historians believe the age on the sarcophagus is incorrect given that it was carved many years later.

Daughter Mary Telfair (1791–1875) outlived her siblings and, upon her death, donated her Savannah home as the first public art museum in the South, now a complex of buildings known as the Telfair Museums. She also endowed the founding of the Telfair Hospital for Females. Today, it continues as Mary Telfair Women's Hospital.

After Mary Telfair's death, St. James Square in Savannah, near the Telfair Museums, was renamed to Telfair Square in honor of the family.

Mary Telfair

George Walton
1749? – 1804

The Orphaned Founder

Buried at Courthouse Grounds,
Augusta, Georgia.

Declaration of Independence

This founder was orphaned at a young age. Many signers of the Declaration of Independence served in state militias, but few participated in any battles during the Revolutionary War. Not only did this founder see action, but he was wounded, captured, and imprisoned by the British. In addition to serving in the Continental Congress, he would also serve as governor and a United States senator from Georgia. His name was George Walton.

Walton was born in Cumberland County, Virginia. The exact year of his birth is unknown. The *New Georgia Encyclopedia* states that it is believed he was born in 1749; however, some researchers have placed his birth as early as 1740. What is known is that he was orphaned at a young age and adopted by an uncle who apprenticed Walton to a carpenter.

Like the date of his birth, there is confusion about his experience as an apprentice. In their book, *Signing Their Lives Away,* Denise Kiernan and Joseph D'Agnese write that there are two stories about how the carpenter treated him. One describes the carpenter as a mean man who was against Walton seeking to educate himself, so he refused to provide a candle so Walton could read his books. In this version, the resourceful Walton

George Walton 1749?–1804

George Walton

gathers wood chips, which he sets ablaze to provide some light to read by. In another, very different version, the carpenter is a kindly gentleman who lets Walton miss work to attend school. The authors conclude that it is difficult to determine which version is accurate, but do note that he was educated enough to study with an attorney when he moved to Savannah, Georgia, in his twenties. He was admitted to the bar in 1774.

Walton became active in supporting the patriots' cause. He was elected secretary of the Georgia Provincial Congress and became president of the Council of Safety. However, his views did not represent those in the majority in Georgia, as evidenced by the fact that Georgia was the only colony that did not send representatives to the First Continental Congress.

It was only when armed conflict between the colonists and the English ensued that the tide turned in Georgia. In 1775, the colony sent delegates to Philadelphia, and in 1776, Walton was elected to join them. Here, he joined Lyman Hall and Button Gwinnett, both considered to be more radical than he was. He would serve honorably and remain in Congress longer than his two colleagues and fellow signers of the Declaration of Independence. If you believe the account of signer Benjamin Rush, Walton was the youngest signer. Rush wrote, "He (Walton) was the youngest member of Congress, not quite being three and twenty when he signed the Declaration of Independence." Thus, Rush added to the possible year of Walton's birth, 1753. However, without additional evidence, the youngest signer must continue to be recognized as Edward Rutledge of South Carolina.

The Signers' Monument in Augusta, Georgia, honors three patriots.

George Walton 1749?–1804

Grave of George Walton

Walton took leave from Congress in 1778 to assume the role of colonel in the militia and fight in the Revolution. During the siege of Savannah, he was shot and fell off his horse. The British quickly captured him. He was not treated harshly and was permitted to seek private medical care to treat the wound in his thigh. Some speculate that the reason for this is that he was a prized prisoner due to his service in Congress and could be used in a prisoner exchange for a high-ranking British officer. He was held prisoner for a year before being exchanged for an English naval captain.

After leaving Congress, Walton continued to serve the people of Georgia as the state's chief justice, governor, and United States senator. He was elected to serve as a delegate to the 1787 Constitutional Convention but declined due to his duties at the state level. In 1789, he served as a presidential elector. He was also the founder and trustee of the Academy of Richmond County in Augusta and of Franklin College, now the University of Georgia in Athens. After serving as governor, he became a judge of the superior court from 1790 until his death.

Walton died in 1804 and was originally buried in Augusta's Rosney Cemetery. His remains were later reinterred in 1848 beneath the signer's monument on the approach to the Augusta municipal building. Lyman Hall is also buried here, and Button Gwinnett is memorialized.

Joseph Wood
(1712–1791)

Pennsylvania Transplant

Burial location unknown,
Sunbury, Georgia.

Continental Congress • Military

Joseph Wood was a Pennsylvanian who moved to Georgia as a young man. When Georgia hesitated to join with the other twelve colonies in revolt, Wood joined the Continental Army in Pennsylvania and rose to the rank of colonel. When Georgia entered the fray, he returned to his new state and was selected to the Continental Congress.

Wood was born circa 1712 in Pennsylvania. His precise lineage is unknown. He likely had a military background.

On December 10, 1747, he received 200 acres of land in Georgia. Around this time, he married Catholena (or Catherine) Reading, likely a native of Delaware born circa 1730. The couple had six children, including Henry (1754), Joseph (1760), John (1762), Hester (1765), Elizabeth (1765), and Jacob (1768), all of whom lived in Georgia.

Through 1770, Wood was listed as living in Savannah, Georgia, west of Bull Street near the wharf. He likely also owned a plantation in what is now the ghost town of Sunbury, Georgia, in St. John's Parish (now Liberty County), about thirty-five miles southwest. Wood was listed as living in Sunbury in 1774.

Joseph Wood (1712–1791)

As the Revolution was underway, Wood was a leading voice for liberty. When the colony of Georgia did not immediately join the other twelve colonies in the First Continental Congress on August 10, 1774, the following February, Wood, Daniel Roberts, and Samuel Stevens requested to join with the South Carolinians in implementing the Continental Association, which involved boycotting British goods.

Frustrated by the lack of movement in his adopted state, Wood returned to Pennsylvania to fight. He was appointed to the rank of major and then rose to lieutenant colonel and then colonel in the 2nd Pennsylvania Regiment led by Arthur St. Clair. Wood saw action in June 1776 with General Sullivan in Canada at Trois-Rivières and in October 1776, when he was wounded at Lake Champlain.

On November 9, 1776, a Philadelphia newspaper referred to Colonel Joseph Wood, in charge of the 3rd Regiment of twelve Pennsylvania regiments in the Continental Army.

On June 7, 1777, Georgia appointed Wood to the Continental Congress. He joined the Congress in York from November 17, 1777, until February 27, 1778. He was again elected on February 26, 1778, but in his 66th year, he returned to Georgia, where he served on the Georgia Council of Safety.

Wood lived the rest of his life on his plantation in Sunbury, Georgia. He died there on October 2, 1791. His burial location has been lost.

Sources

Books, Magazines, Journals, Files:

Alexander, Edward P. *Revolutionary Conservative: James Duane of New York*. New York: Ams Press, 1978.

Anthony, Katharine Susan. *First Lady of the Revolution; The Life of Mercy Otis Warren*. Port Washington, N.Y.: Kennikat Press, 1972.

Appleby, Joyce. *Inheriting the Revolution: The First Generation of Americans*. Cambridge, Massachusetts: Harvard University Press, 2000.

Atkinson, Rick. *The British Are Coming: The War for America, Lexington to Princeton, 1775–1777*. New York: Henry Holt & Co. 2019.

Bordewich, Fergus M. *The First Congress: How James Madison, George Washington, and a Group of Extraordinary Men Invented the Government*. New York: Simon and Schuster Paperbacks, 2016.

Boudreau, George W. *Independence: A Guide to Historic Philadelphia*. Yardley, Pennsylvania: Westholme Publishing, LLC. 2012.

Bowen, Catherine Drinker. *Miracle at Philadelphia: The Story of the Constitutional Convention May to September 1787*. Boston, Massachusetts: Little, Brown & Company, 1966.

Breen, T.H, *George Washington's Journey: The President Forges a New Nation*. New York: Simon & Schuster. 2016.

Brookhiser, Richard. *Gentleman Revolutionary: Gouverneur Morris The Rake Who Wrote the Constitution*. New York: Free Press, 2003.

———. *John Marshall: The Man Who Made the Supreme Court*. New York: Basic Books. 2018.

Brush, Edward Hale. *Rufus King and His Times*. New York: N.L. Brown, 1926.

Chadwick, Bruce. I Am Murdered: *George Wythe, Thomas Jefferson, and the Killing That Shocked a New Nation*. Hoboken, New Jersey: John Wiley & Sons, 2009.

Chambers, II, John Whiteclay. *The Oxford Companion to American Military History*. Oxford: Oxford University Press, 1999.

Commager, Henry Steele & Richard B. Morris. *The Spirit of 'Seventy-Six: The Story of the American Revolution as Told by Participants*. New York: Harper & Rowe, 1967.

Cole, Ryan. *Light-Horse Harry Lee: The Rise and Fall of a Revolutionary Hero*. Washington, D.C.: Regnery History. 2019.

Conlin, Joseph R. *The Morrow Book of Quotations in American History*. New York: William Morrow and Company, Inc., 1984.

Daniels, Jonathan. *Ordeal of Ambition*. Garden City, New York: Doubleday & Company, Inc., 1970.

Dann, John C. *The Revolution Remembered: Eyewitness Accounts of the War for Independence*. Chicago: University of Chicago Press, 1980.

SOURCES

DeRose, Chris. *Founding Rivals: Madison vs. Monroe: The Bill of Rights and the Election that Saved a Nation.* New York: MJF Books, 2011.

Drury, Bob & Tom Clavin. *Valley Forge.* New York: Simon & Schuster. 2018.

Ellis, Joseph J. *Revolutionary Summer: The Birth of American Independence.* New York: Alfred A. Knopf, 2013.

———. *The Quartet: Orchestrating the Second American Revolution, 1783–1789.* New York: Alfred A. Knopf, 2015.

———. *His Excellency: George Washington.* New York: Alfred A. Knopf, 2004.

Flexner, James Thomas. *George Washington in the American Revolution, 1775–1783.* Boston: Little, Brown & Company, 1967.

Flower, Lenore Embick. "Visit of President George Washington to Carlisle, 1794." Carlisle, Pennsylvania: The Hamilton Library and Cumberland County Historical Society, 1932.

Gerlach, Don R. *Proud Patriot: Philip Schuyler and the War of Independence, 1775–1783.* Syracuse, N.Y.: Syracuse University Press, 1987.

Goodrich, Charles A. *Lives of the Signers of the Declaration of Independence.* Charlotteville, N.Y.: SamHar Press, 1976.

Griffith, IV, William R. *The Battle of Lake George: England's First Triumph in the French and Indian War.* Charleston, South Carolina: The History Press, 2016.

Grossman, Mark. *Encyclopedia of the Continental Congress.* Armenia, New York: Grey House Publishing, 2015.

Hamilton, Edward P. *Fort Ticonderoga: Key to a Continent.* Boston: Little, Brown & Company, 1964.

Isenberg, Nancy. *Fallen Founder: The Life of Aaron Burr.* New York: Penguin Group, 2007.

Kennedy, Roger G. *Burr, Hamilton, and Jefferson: A Study in Character.* New York: Oxford University Press, 1999.

Kiernan, Denise & Joseph D'Agnese. *Signing Their Lives Away: The Fame and Misfortune of the Men Who Signed the Declaration of Independence.* Philadelphia: Quirk Books, 2008.

———. *Signing Their Rights Away: The Fame and Misfortune of the Men Who Signed the United States Constitution.* Philadelphia: Quirk Books, 2011.

Klarman, Michael J. *The Framers' Coup: The Making of the United States Constitution.* New York: Oxford University Press, 2016.

Langguth, A. J. *Patriots.* New York: Simon and Schuster, 1988.

Larson, Edward J. *A Magnificient Catastrophe.* New York: Free Press, 2007.

Lee, Mike. Written *Out of History: The Forgotten Founders Who Fought Big Government.* New York: Penguin Books, 2017.

Lewis, James E., Jr., *The Burr Conspiracy: Uncovering the Story of an Early American Crisis*, Princeton: Princeton University Press, 2017.

Lockridge, Ross Franklin. *The Harrisons.* 1941.

Lomask, Milton. *Aaron Burr: The Years from Princeton to Vice President, 1756–1805.* New York: Farrar Straus Giroux, 1979.

Lossing, Benson J. *Pictorial Field Book of the Revolution.* New York: Harper Brothers. 1851.

Maier, Pauline. *American Scripture: Making the Declaration of Independence*. New York: Alfred A. Knopf, Inc., 1997.

McCullough, David. *John Adams*. New York: Simon & Schuster, 2002.

Meltzer, Brad & Josh Mensch. *The First Conspiracy: The Secret Plot to Kill George Washington*. New York: Flat Iron Books. 2018.

Middlekauff, Robert. *The Glorious Cause: The American Revolution, 1763–1789*. Oxford: Oxford University Press, 2005.

Miller, Jr., Arthur P. & Marjorie L. Miller. *Pennsylvania Battlefields and Military Landmarks*. Mechanicsburg, Pennsylvania: Stackpole Books, 2000.

Millett, Allan R. & Peter Maslowski. *For the Common Defense: A Military History of the United States of America*. New York: The Free Press, 1984.

Moore, Charles. *The Family Life of George Washington*. New York: Houghton Mifflin, 1926.

Nagel, Paul C. *The Lees of Virginia: Seven Generations of an American Family*. Oxford: Oxford University Press, 1990.

O'Connell, Robert L. *Revolutionary: George Washington at War*. New York: Random House. 2019.

Racove, Jack N. *Revolutionaries: A New History of the Invention of America*. New York: Houghton Mifflin Harcourt, 2011.

Raphael, Ray. *Founding Myths: Stories That Hide Our Patriotic Past*. New York: MJF Books, 2004.

Rossiter, Clinton. *1787 The Grand Convention*. New York: The Macmillan Company, 1966.

Seymour, Joseph. *The Pennsylvania Associators, 1747–1777*. Yardley, Pennsylvania: Westholme Publishing, LLC. 2012.

Schweikart, Larry & Michael Allen. *A Patriot's History of the United States from Columbus's Great Discovery to the War on Terror*. New York: Penguin, 2004.

Sharp, Arthur G. *Not Your Father's Founders*. Avon, Massachusetts: Adams Media, 2012.

Stahr, Walter. *John Jay: Founding Father*. New York: Diversion Books, 2017.

Taafee, Stephen R. *The Philadelphia Campaign, 1777–1778*. Lawrence, Kansas: University of Kansas Press, 2003.

Tinkcom, Harry Marlin, *The Republicans and the Federalists in Pennsylvania, 1790–1801*. Harrisburg, Pennsylvania: Pennsylvania Historical and Museum Commission. 1950.

Ward, Matthew C. *Breaking the Backcountry: The Seven Years' War in Virginia and Pennsylvania, 1754–1765*. Pittsburgh, Pennsylvania: University of Pittsburgh Press, 2003.

Weisberger, Bernard A. *America Afire: Jefferson, Adams, and the Revolutionary Election of 1800*. New York: HarperCollins, 2000.

Wood, Gordon S. *The Radicalism of the American Revolution*. New York: Vintage Books, 1993.

———. *Empire of Liberty: A History of the Early Republic, 1789–1815*. New York: Penguin Books, 2004.

———. *Revolutionary Characters: What Made the Founders Different*. New York: Penguin Books, 2006.

SOURCES

———. *The Americanization of Benjamin Franklin*. Oxford: Oxford University Press, 2009.

Wright, Benjamin F. *The Federalist: The Famous Papers on the Principles of American Government: Alexander Hamilton, James Madison, John Jay*. New York: Metro Books, 2002.

Zobel, Hiller B. *The Boston Massacre*. New York: W. W. Norton & Company, 1970.

Video Resources:

Guelzo, Allen C. The Great Courses: *America's Founding Fathers* (Course N. 8525). Chantilly, Virginia: The Teaching Company, 2017.

Online Resources:

Archives.gov – for information on the Constitutional Convention.
CauseofLiberty.blogspot.com – for information on Daniel Carroll.
ColonialHall.com – for information about the signers of the Declaration of Independence.
DSDI1776.com – for information on many Founders.
FamousAmericans.net – for information on many Founders.
FindaGrave.com – for burial information, vital statistics and obituaries.
FirstLadies.org – for information on Abigail Adams.
Newspapers.com – Hundreds of newspaper articles were accessed—too numerous to mention here.
NPS.gov – for information on various park sites.
TeachingAmericanHistory.com – for information on Charles Pinckney and George Wythe.
TheHistoryJunkie.com – for information on multiple Founders.
USHistory.org – for information on multiple Founders.
Wikipedia.com – for general historical information.

Index

Adams, John, 3, 5
Articles of Confederation, vi, 35–36, 38–40
Athens, Georgia, 10, 15
Augusta, Georgia, 7, 12, 15, 17, 19, 30–31, 34, 42, 44–45
Bulloch, Archibald, v, 1–5, 28
Baldwin, Abraham, vi, 6–10
Boston, Massachusetts, 21
Brownson, Nathan, v, 11–14
Charleston, South Carolina, 1, 23, 26
Constitution, US, vi, 6, 9, 15, 18, 40
Continental Association, 3, 32, 47
Declaration of Independence, v, 5, 26–28, 30–31, 34, 36, 42, 44
Elbert, Samuel, 40
Few, William, vi, 9, 15–19
Georgia, University of, 6, 8, 10, 13, 18, 34, 45
Greene, Nathanael, v, 7, 13, 17, 20–25
Gwinnett, Button, v, 26–30, 36, 43, 45
Hall, Lyman, v, 7, 11–12, 27, 29, 31–34, 43, 45
Hamilton, Alexander, 18
Hancock, John, 5
Heard, Stephen, 12
Houston, John, 2
Houston, William, 9
Jefferson, Thomas, 18
Jones, Wimberly, 2
Langworthy, Edward, vi, 35–37, 39
Martin, John, 13
Mathews, George, 40
McIntosh, Lachlan, 3, 28–29
New York, New York, 17–19, 22, 30, 37
Pendleton, Nathaniel, 9
Philadelphia, Pennsylvania, 2, 5, 12, 18, 22, 25, 33, 36, 39, 43, 47
Pierce, William, 9, 18
Roosevelt, Eleanor, 1, 5
Roosevelt, Theordore, 1, 5
Savannah, Georgia, v, 1-3, 5, 11, 17, 20, 23–24, 26–29, 33, 35–36, 38–39, 41, 43, 45–46
Telfair, Edward, v–vi, 38–41
Walton, George, v, 2–3, 9, 29, 40, 42–45
Washington, George, 20–24, 29
Wood, Joseph, 46–47
Wright, Sir James, v, 2–3
York, Pennsylvania, 12, 36, 40, 48
Zubly, John Joachim, 3

www.ingramcontent.com/pod-product-compliance
Lightning Source LLC
Chambersburg PA
CBHW011802040426
42449CB00016B/3467